D1709482

GHOST STORIES

GHOSTS IN MANSIONS

By Lisa Owings

Jessamine County Public Library
600 South Main Street
Nicholasville, KY 40356

EPIC

BELLWETHER MEDIA • MINNEAPOLIS, MN

EPIC BOOKS are no ordinary books. They burst with intense action, high-speed heroics, and shadows of the unknown. Are you ready for an Epic adventure?

This edition first published in 2017 by Bellwether Media, Inc.

No part of this publication may be reproduced in whole or in part without written permission of the publisher.
For information regarding permission, write to Bellwether Media, Inc., Attention: Permissions Department,
5357 Penn Avenue South, Minneapolis, MN 55419.

Library of Congress Cataloging-in-Publication Data

Names: Owings, Lisa, author.
Title: Ghosts in Mansions / by Lisa Owings.
Description: Minneapolis, MN : Bellwether Media, Inc., [2017] | Series: Epic.
   Ghost Stories | Audience: Ages 7-12. | Audience: Grades 2 to 7. |
   Includes bibliographical references and index.
Identifiers: LCCN 2016005077 | ISBN 9781626174290 (hardcover : alk. paper)
Subjects: LCSH: Haunted houses–Juvenile literature. | Ghosts–Juvenile
   literature.
Classification: LCC BF1475 .O95 2017 | DDC 133.1/22–dc23
LC record available at http://lccn.loc.gov/2016005077

Text copyright © 2017 by Bellwether Media, Inc. EPIC and associated logos are trademarks and/or registered trademarks of Bellwether Media, Inc. SCHOLASTIC, CHILDREN'S PRESS, and associated logos are trademarks and/or registered trademarks of Scholastic Inc.

Printed in the United States of America, North Mankato, MN.

TABLE OF CONTENTS

HAUNTED MANSIONS

You are **admiring** a room in an old mansion. Then, you see your tour group has moved on. You are alone. *Slam!* The door shuts and locks. Has a spirit trapped you here?

A HOUSE FOR WANDERING SPIRITS

Winchester Mystery House is in California. Its construction began in the 1800s. Stories say Sarah Winchester built the house to confuse spirits.

Winchester
Mystery House,
California

N
W ✦ E
S

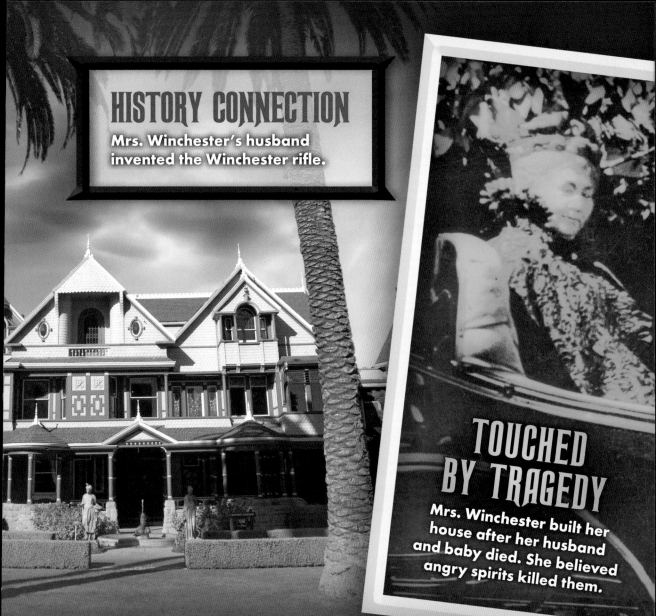

HISTORY CONNECTION
Mrs. Winchester's husband invented the Winchester rifle.

TOUCHED BY TRAGEDY
Mrs. Winchester built her house after her husband and baby died. She believed angry spirits killed them.

Its stairs go down, then up. The hallways twist and turn. Secret passages and sealed rooms hide behind walls.

Today, the house hosts tours. At one point, staff began to notice a man in the basement. He had a mustache and wore white overalls. He also pushed a wheelbarrow. Everyone thought he worked there.

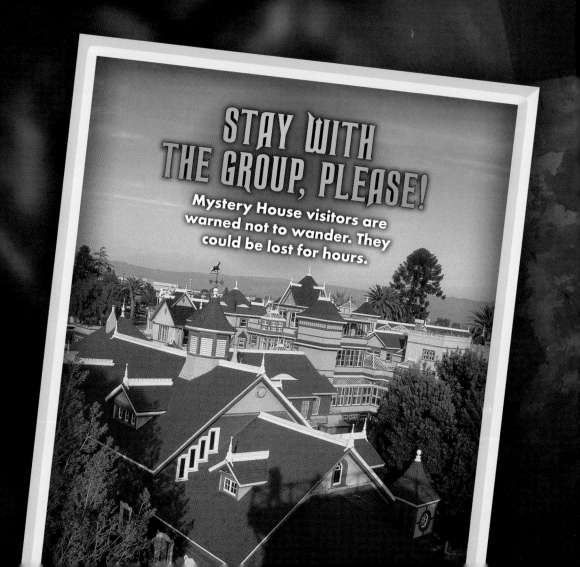

STAY WITH THE GROUP, PLEASE!

Mystery House visitors are warned not to wander. They could be lost for hours.

Later, a guest found an old photo. It showed the home's builders. One was the man with the mustache! Has he continued working, even after death?

UNFINISHED BUSINESS

Mrs. Winchester never stopped work on her house. Over 38 years, 500 or more rooms were built. Only 160 remain.

SIGHTINGS AT THE WINCHESTER
MYSTERY HOUSE

- All lights on the third floor turning on when the house was empty

- Tour guide hearing someone call her name, though guests said nothing

- Man from an old photo appearing several times in the basement

- Woman dressed like Mrs. Winchester sitting in the dining room

- The smell of chicken soup coming from an unused kitchen

A POLTERGEIST'S PRISON

The Borley **Rectory** was built in England in 1863. A **monastery** once stood there. Neighbors warned that the site was haunted.

Borley Rectory,
England

People often saw the ghost of a nun. She walked outside or stared through windows.

Legend says a **monk** had a **forbidden** romance with a nun. The monk was killed. The nun was sealed alive in the walls of her **convent**.

HISTORY CONNECTION

In the 1930s, ghost hunter Harry Price searched the house. He later claimed to have found the ghostly nun's bones.

A BONE-CHILLING FIND

One woman found a package while cleaning the rectory. Inside was a human skull.

Over the years, several families lived in the rectory. None stayed for long.

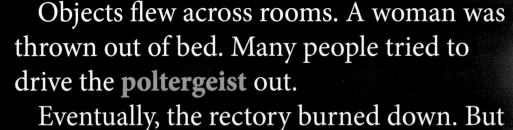

Objects flew across rooms. A woman was thrown out of bed. Many people tried to drive the **poltergeist** out.

Eventually, the rectory burned down. But the grounds are still said to be haunted.

SIGHTINGS AT THE BORLEY RECTORY

- **Nun strolling the grounds**
- **Horse-drawn carriage pulling up the drive**
- **Messages on walls asking for help**
- **Objects thrown at people in the house**
- **Girl locked in room that had no key**

HELP ME!

Written messages appeared on the walls. They seemed to be from a spirit asking for help. Most were unreadable.

EXPLAINING THE UNEXPLAINED?

Mrs. Winchester lost her whole family. **Skeptics** say building her mansion helped her **cope**. They say the spirits are just a story.

Others believe the ghost stories
are true. Visitors often claim to spot
ghosts themselves.

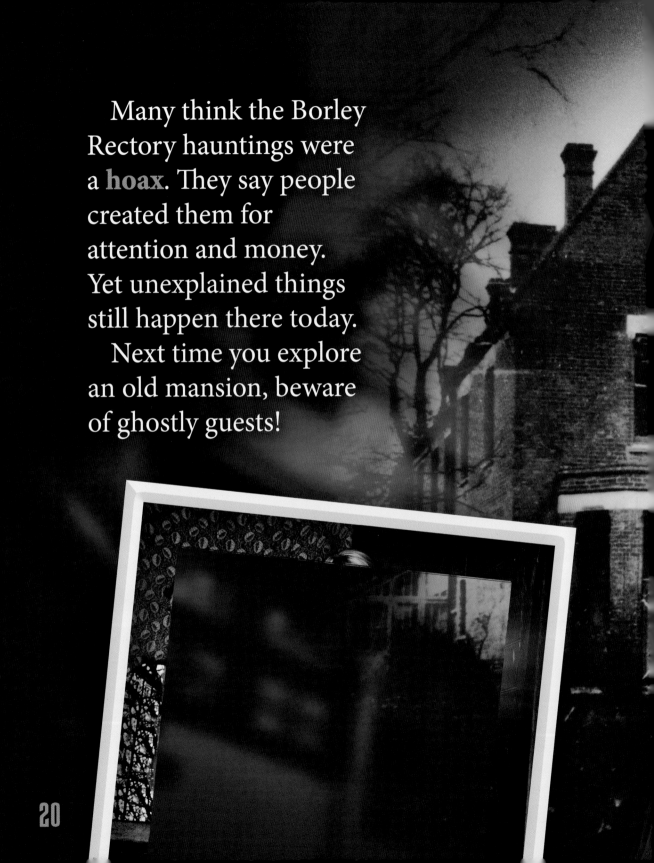

Many think the Borley Rectory hauntings were a **hoax**. They say people created them for attention and money. Yet unexplained things still happen there today.

Next time you explore an old mansion, beware of ghostly guests!

GLOSSARY

admiring—looking at with enjoyment

convent—a building where nuns live

cope—to deal with and overcome problems or difficulties

forbidden—not allowed

hoax—a trick to make someone believe something that is not true

legend—a story many believe that has not been proven true

monastery—a building where monks live

monk—a man who lives apart from other people because of religious beliefs; monks have many rules that they must follow.

poltergeist—an invisible ghost that scares people by making noise and moving objects

rectory—the home of the head of a church

skeptics—people who doubt the truth of something

TO LEARN MORE

AT THE LIBRARY

Higgins, Nadia. *Ghosts*. Minneapolis, Minn.: Bellwether Media, 2014.

Higgins, Nadia. *Haunted Houses*. Minneapolis, Minn.: Bellwether Media, 2014.

Perish, Patrick. *Are Haunted Houses Real?* Mankato, Minn.: Amicus High Interest, 2014.

ON THE WEB

Learning more about ghosts in mansions is as easy as 1, 2, 3.

1. Go to www.factsurfer.com.

2. Enter "ghosts in mansions" into the search box.

3. Click the "Surf" button and you will see a list of related web sites.

With factsurfer.com, finding more information is just a click away.

INDEX

The images in this book are reproduced through the courtesy of: Herb Klein, front cover (ghost face); Serg Zastavkin, front cover (ghost body), p. 19 (ghost); Citizen of the Planet/ SuperStock, front cover (background), pp. 1, 6-7; Marcos Mesa Sam Wordley, pp. 4-5; PhotoStock-Israel/ Alamy, pp. 4-5 (background), 11; Bettmann/ Corbis, p. 7; Robert Holmes/ Corbis, p. 8; bikeriderlondon, p. 9 (ghost); wiktord, p. 9 (background); MCT/ Getty Images, p. 10 (house); Masterovoy, p. 10 (wheelbarrow); Mary Evans Picture Library/ Age Fotostock, pp. 13, 17 (messages); shipfactory, pp. 14 (woman), 21 (ghost); GoneWithTheWind, p. 14 (background); HABRDA, p. 15 (skull); Gilmanshin, p. 15 (background); Mary Evans Picture Library/ HARRY PRICE/ Age Fotostock, p. 16; Phillip Bond/ Alamy, p. 18; Poprotskiy Alexey, p. 19 (hand); John Pyle/ Cal Sport Media/ Newscom, p. 19 (room); Jandrie Lombard, p. 20; The Marsden Archive/ Alamy, p. 21 (background).